Weather Update

Wind

by Terri Sievert

Consultant:
Joseph M. Moran, PhD
Associate Director, Education Program
American Meteorological Society, Washington, D.C.

Capstone press

Mankato, Minnesota

Bridgestone Books are published by Capstone Press,
151 Good Counsel Drive, P.O. Box 669, Mankato, Minnesota 56002.
www.capstonepress.com

Library of Congress Cataloging-in-Publication Data
Sievert, Terri.
    Wind / by Terri Sievert.
        p. cm.—(Bridgestone books. Weather update)
    Includes bibliographical references and index.
    ISBN 0-7368-3740-X (hardcover)
    1. Winds—Juvenile literature. I. Title. II. Series.
QC981.3.S54 2005
551.51'8—dc22   2004010858

Summary: Discusses wind and how it affects the weather.

Editorial Credits
Christopher Harbo, editor; Molly Nei, set designer; Ted Williams, illustrator;
    Wanda Winch, photo researcher; Scott Thoms, photo editor

Photo Credits
Capstone Press/Karon Dubke, 1
Corbis/Annie Griffiths Belt, 18; Jay Syverson, 4; Wolfgang Kaehler, 10
Corbis Sygma, 20
Dan Delaney Photography, cover (child), back cover
EyeWire (Photodisc), 6
Getty Images Inc./Stone, 12; Terry Qing, cover (background)
Tom Pantages, 14, 16

1 2 3 4 5 6 10 09 08 07 06 05

Table of Contents

What Is Wind?

A light breeze stirs the leaves on a tree. A wind gust lifts a kite high in the sky. A blast of wind makes snow swirl.

Wind is the natural movement of the air. It can be light or strong. Wind can cool you down or blow you over. You can't see the wind, but you can see what it does. You feel it hit your face. You hear it rattle your windows. Wind is a powerful force that changes the weather.

◄ A strong ocean wind lifts kites high in the sky.

How Wind Forms

Wind is moving air. Heat from the sun helps air start moving. Sunlight warms the ground. The ground warms the air above the earth's surface unevenly.

Wind forms when cool air meets warm air. Cool air is heavier than warm air. The cool air pushes under the warm air, and the wind begins to blow.

◄ Fluffy seeds ride a light breeze on a warm autumn day.

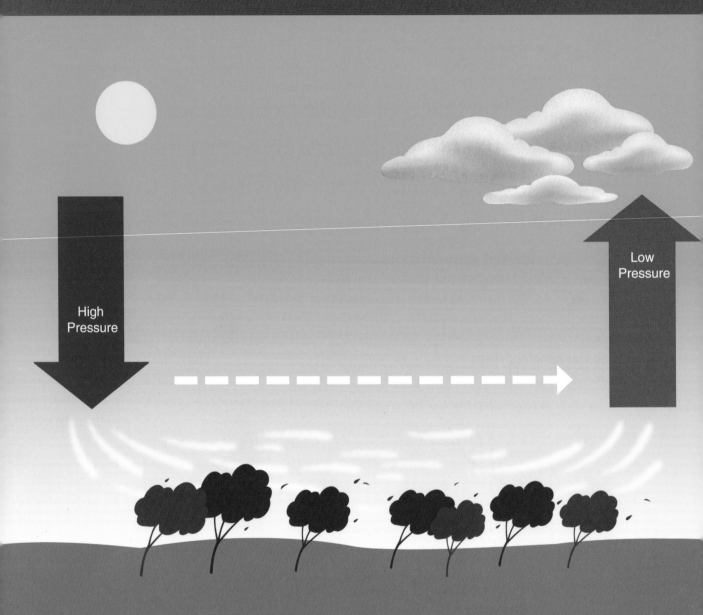

High Pressure

Low Pressure

Air Pressure

Air presses down on the earth. The weight of air above an area of the earth's surface is called **air pressure**.

A **mass** of cooler air produces high air pressure. A mass of warmer air produces low air pressure. Wind blows from high air pressure toward low air pressure.

Scientists use **barometers** to measure air pressure. This instrument shows the weight of the air in an area. Barometers show when air pressure is rising and falling.

◀ Wind blows from areas of high pressure to areas of low pressure.

10

Wind Direction

A weather vane shows the direction of the wind. Many weather vanes have an arrow connected to a rod. The directions for north, south, west, and east are below the arrow. When the wind blows, the arrow turns. The arrow points in the direction the wind is coming from.

In the United States, wind usually blows from southwest to northeast. Warm winds blow from the south and southwest. Cool winds come from the north and northwest.

◄ The weather vane's arrow is pointing between south and east. The wind is blowing from the southeast.

Wind Speed

Wind speeds are measured in miles or kilometers per hour. The number of miles or kilometers air travels in one hour is the wind speed.

Wind speeds change with the weather. A gentle breeze blows at about 8 miles (13 kilometers) per hour. People have a hard time walking against a wind blowing 38 miles (61 kilometers) per hour. Strong thunderstorms can have wind gusts over 70 miles (113 kilometers) per hour.

◀ Some winds are so strong a person can lean into them and not fall over.

Measuring Wind Speed

Scientists use an **anemometer** to measure wind speed. This instrument has three or four cups attached to a spoke. The spoke turns as the wind blows the cups. A switch counts how many times the spoke turns.

An **aerovane** is also used to measure wind speed. It looks like a small airplane. It has a **propeller** on one end. The propeller turns as the wind blows. A computer counts the turns to measure wind speed.

◄ A scientist checks an aerovane to see how fast the wind is blowing.

What Is Wind Chill?

Wind chill is how cold the air feels on a windy day. Wind blows heat away from your body. It makes your body feel colder. A strong wind can make a sunny winter day feel very cold.

Scientists use a wind chill **index** to find out how cold the air feels. This chart combines temperature and wind speed to measure wind chill.

◄ A scientist reads a wind chill index on his computer to find out the wind chill temperature.

Gales and Hurricanes

Winds can be powerful. A gale is a very strong wind. It blows between 32 and 54 miles (51 and 87 kilometers) per hour. Large trees blow over in the strongest gales. Gales can also damage buildings.

Hurricane winds are even stronger than gales. A hurricane forms over warm ocean water. The storm swirls around a center point called an eye. Hurricane winds blow 74 miles (119 kilometers) per hour or faster. Hurricanes near land can destroy homes and cause floods.

◀ Powerful hurricane winds blow large waves against houses near the ocean.

Using Wind to Predict Weather

Forecasters look at wind direction when predicting the weather. In North America, northwest winds often bring clear skies and cooler temperatures. Wind blowing from the southwest usually brings fair weather. An approaching storm may cause winds to blow from the south, southeast, or east.

Check the wind outside today. Which way is it blowing? Does it feel strong or light? What kind of weather do you think the wind is bringing to your area?

◀ A scientist measures wind speed with an anemometer during a tropical storm.

Glossary

aerovane (AIR-oh-vayn)—an instrument with a spinning propeller that measures wind speed

air pressure (AIR PRESH-ur)—the weight of air on a surface

anemometer (an-i-MOM-uh-tur)—an instrument with spinning cups that measures wind speed

barometer (buh-ROM-uh-tur)—an instrument that measures changes in air pressure

forecaster (FOR-kast-ur)—a person who predicts the weather

index (IN-deks)—a list or chart; a wind chill index is a chart that combines air temperature and wind speed.

mass (MASS)—a pile or collection of matter that has no particular shape

propeller (pruh-PEL-ur)—a set of rotating blades; an aerovane uses a propeller to measure wind speed.

Read More

Bauer, Marion Dane. *Wind.* Ready-to-Read. New York: Aladdin, 2003.

Miles, Elizabeth. *Wind.* Watching the Weather. Chicago: Heinemann, 2005.

Internet Sites

FactHound offers a safe, fun way to find Internet sites related to this book. All of the sites on FactHound have been researched by our staff.

Here's how:
1. Visit *www.facthound.com*
2. Type in this special code **073683740X** for age-appropriate sites. Or enter a search word related to this book for a more general search.
3. Click on the **Fetch It** button.

FactHound will fetch the best sites for you!

Index